MICROCOSM PUBLISHING is Portland's most diversified publishing house and distributor, with a focus on the colorful, authentic, and empowering. Our books and zines have put your power in your hands since 1996, equipping readers to make positive changes in their lives and in the world around them. Microcosm emphasizes skill-building, showing hidden histories, and fostering creativity through challenging conventional publishing wisdom with books and bookettes about DIY skills, food, bicycling, gender, self-care, and social justice. What was once a distro and record label started by Joe Biel in a drafty bedroom was determined to be *Publishers Weekly*'s fastest-growing publisher of 2022 and #3 in 2023 and 2024, and is now among the oldest independent publishing houses in Portland, OR, and Cleveland, OH. We are a politically moderate, centrist publisher in a world that has inched to the right for the past 80 years.

CONTENTS

Dedication • 5

Introduction • 6

Chapter 1: On Aging • 9

Chapter 2: Personal Values • 11

Chapter 3: Values in a Love Relationship • 13

Chapter 4: Who Were You? • 16

Chapter 5: Your Brave Self • 18

Chapter 6: Your Fearful Self • 20

Chapter 7: Transition • 22

Chapter 8: Dare to Dream • 26

Chapter 9: Choices • 29

Chapter 10: Boundaries • 31

Chapter 11: Developing Friendships • 34

Chapter 12: Intimacy and Sex • 37

Chapter 13: Limiting Beliefs • 40

Chapter 14: Forgiveness • 42

Chapter 15: Positive Thinking • 44

Chapter 16: The Art of Play • 46

Chapter 17: Setting Intentions and Manifesting Them • 49

Chapter 18: Some Final Thoughts for Those Over 70! • 52

About the Author • 56

Acknowledgements • 57

DEDICATION

While I was writing this, a very positive person I knew, Doug Dickie, died. I met him in 2010, and he eventually became a good friend of mine. Doug was diagnosed with rheumatoid arthritis at the age of eighteen, and, over the years, he had many joints in his body replaced because of the crippling disease. It never stopped him from doing anything he wanted to do. He was a downhill skier, curler, swimmer, hiker, golfer, business owner, and world traveler.

Just before he passed, at the age of 76, Doug was waiting "impatiently" for a 3D shoulder replacement so he could continue doing everything he loved. He lived his life to the fullest, was there for both old and new friends, tried to learn something new every day, and found laughter a necessary part of life. He didn't sit on the couch when he retired but kept doing all the things he loved to do for as long as he could do them. He learned *How to Age (in Style!)*.

INTRODUCTION

You are always growing and changing, mentally, emotionally, and physically, whether you are eight or eighty. Some people at age forty are already worrying that by the time they are eighty, they will be dealing with Alzheimer's or dementia. If you are doing that, you are worrying about something that may never happen. Why?

Does a person reach a certain age where they are considered "old"? Many countries around the world have set a retirement age at 65, at which time a person can draw a social security or state pension. In Canada, the government retirement pension is called Old Age Security and can also be applied for at the age of 65. Ageism is already in place in that country. "Senior" is another term that is used in the United States and Canada and allows for retail discounts for people from the age of 55 and up, so the age of being old is even younger!

Andrew Steele, in his book *Ageless*, writes about getting older without getting old. Is that even possible with the government and media telling people they are old? The preeminent fashion magazine, *Vogue*, featured a 106-year-old Philippine tattoo artist, Apo Whang-Od, on the April 2023 cover. What if they hadn't said how old she was? Did it matter what her age was? Or was it a marketing ploy now that the UN has announced that 10 percent of the world population of over 8 billion is over 65?

What if you could just be any age, and do it in style, without reference to being young or old or anywhere in between? According to investment research platform MacroTrends, life expectancy in the United States in 2024 is currently 79.25 years, while in Canada, the life expectancy is 83.11 years. Steele said, "We are in the age of aging." Many people will look at careers and retirement much differently now because the years of productivity have increased substantially in the last fifty years. There is no reason to consider yourselves as being old nor is there a reason that you can't work up until the time you die. People might want to leave their jobs early, travel while they are physically active, and then return to work later in life.

From the day you are born, you are aging. What you learn to believe in the first eight years of your life is controlled by the adults around you, parents, grandparents, neighbors, and teachers. As you grow beyond eight, you begin to develop critical and abstract thinking skills, and your peers have much more influence on what you believe. The behavior of an adolescent who is a risk-taker may also have a very different life experience than an adolescent who is not. Also, the age of adolescence may expand well beyond the teenage years.

According to an article published by the NIH National Library of Medicine titled "Maturation of the Adolescent Brain" (Arain et al., 2013), the brain goes through rewiring during adolescence and the process isn't complete until around the age of 25. The prefrontal cortex (one of the last regions of the brain to reach maturation) is responsible for cognitive analysis, abstract thought, and the ability to use correct behavior in social situations. This explains why some 22-year-olds are still not mature.

The subject of brain development is very interesting and complex, but this zine is not about how the brain develops.

The following pages are about how to age in style, enjoy every minute of your life, and quit worrying about what is coming next—no matter your age or gender.

Throughout these pages, I will share short stories about the journey that took me and others in different directions from what's considered the norm. It doesn't matter how old you are or even if your family, your spouse, your government, or the niggling voice in your head has told you that you can't do something or accomplish something. Know that you are the one who makes that decision.

At the end of each chapter, there are reflection questions connected to the topic. You can either write your answers to these questions in a separate notebook or just internally reflect on them. The questions will help you look at who you were, who you are right now, as well as who you want to be, no matter your age. Before you continue reading these pages, I hope you will commit to giving yourself 15 minutes a day of reflection time. When you begin, pick a time that resonates with you, whether it be first thing in the morning or last thing at night. This is a time when there is less chance of being interrupted by daily routine, pets, or partners.

It is important to be relaxed when you reflect on each section. I find the best way for me to do this is through a meditation process. There are many free guided meditations available online, or you can simply close your eyes and listen to your favorite calming piece of music.

If you are in a relationship, let your partner know that you are setting aside 15 minutes a day just for you! If you find that isn't agreeable to them, then hopefully the information that you read in the following pages will help you discuss this with them.

What originally inspired me to write this zine was the realization of how many people I know who struggle with change. They had trouble dreaming about what they wanted to do next in life. My formal training was in Human Services, and I worked with the local school district supporting teens with severe physical, mental, and behavioral issues. Outside of work, I volunteered with teenage victims of sexual abuse as well as youth at risk in the justice system. I soon realized that many of the kids I worked with and those I volunteered with had no concept of how to dream. I created a program for them, "Dare to Dream," and thirty years later, I used the same program outline as building blocks for this zine. I also realized by then that some of my peers had reached the age of retirement and either quit dreaming completely or never learned how to dream, just like the youth! I wrote *How to Age (in Style!* to give people the steps needed to achieve their dreams. It is something everyone of us can do if we only take a chance!

CHAPTER 1: ON AGING

*A*n adult just getting their prefrontal cortex working to full capacity might think 45 years old is ancient! If you are in your twenties, less than a third of my age, you know so much more than I ever did at your age because of the way our worlds and the information highway connect now. There might be many people you will meet in your life who always seem old. I still meet people who think the same way they did fifty years ago, and my only advice is: Do not waste your time and energy on those who won't accept change. There are too many others out there in the world who want change to happen.

I also learned a few years ago that I won't give much of my energy to people who have a negative outlook on life. I'm not talking about people in crisis but people who have chosen to complain about the same thing day in and day out and not let those thoughts go. It took me a while to let go of people around me who had so much negative energy, but I eventually learned. With 8 billion people in the world, there are many positive people to pick from, but it required some work on my part!

Disconnecting with others takes time, especially if they are part of your extended family. You can still be a part of the family if you choose and attend family functions, but that doesn't mean you have to accept their beliefs, argue to try to change their minds, or spend time convincing them that they should think differently, although many try. It all has to do with respect, not only respect for others but respect for yourself.

For instance, many people sit around, moaning about the state of the world, waiting to die after they retire instead of grabbing every moment of life. I have heard people say, "I worked hard all my life. I deserve to rest." I will respect a person who wishes to end their life doing that, but I am sad that the route they have chosen leads them to the corner of the couch. How do they age in style doing that? I choose to get up off the couch and participate in life with people who want to do the same!

A Story about Aging

Bronnie Ware is an Australian palliative care nurse who wrote the book, *The Top Five Regrets of the Dying*. She said the most common regret people who are dying have is, "I wish I'd had the courage to live a life true to myself, not the life others expected of me." If you live your life to keep others happy, you are the only one missing out!

The way you "age" is often based on messages that you received when you were a child or teenager, generational messages passed down from grandparents to parents to children. Those messages are probably ingrained in your DNA without you even realizing it. They are the "should" messages: what you should eat, what you should wear, who you should play with, what and who you should grow up to be, what you should spend your money on, what university you should go to, what you should believe in, what career you should have, where you should live, and, in some families, who you should marry. The "should" list can be endless and even when you approach the end of your life, those "should" words continue.

Reflecting on Aging

Reflect on the people you have in your life right now and determine if they are positive or negative influences in your life. Do they take too much of your positive energy for themselves, or do they make you feel good when you are with them? Take 15 minutes to think about this question. Some people find this a good time to begin journaling.

CHAPTER 2: PERSONAL VALUES

*I*t is fine to say don't let go of your values, but what are values? Values are your core beliefs and are the most important things you can discover about yourself at any age. So often you grow up thinking you are the same as everyone in your family, but your thoughts on what is important to you may change as you mature.

Your values will not change unless you look at them closely and you choose to change them. Determining what your values are as an adult is an important part of how to age the best way you can and learn about who you are! Any changes you make in life are usually a result of your values. When your values clash with another person's values it can create issues that can't always be resolved. If you are able, respect each other's way of thinking, but, if you can't, move on and make new friends with like-minded people.

My values will not change unless I choose to change them. Developing a list of my values took time but helped me clarify who I was.

One of my top three values is Making a Difference. I learned early in life that I could make a difference, but the way I went about it was not a popular idea with my parents. When I was ten years old, I collaborated with a nine-year-old friend to collect seashells, glue them on chunks of wood that we painted, and sell them throughout the neighborhood. We then donated the money we made, $35—a huge amount at the time—to an orphan's fund.

My parents were mortified when our names were shared on the local radio station. I learned to keep a lower profile with my endeavors, around my parents anyway! My values were different from theirs, but it would take me years to understand and accept my values as a positive thing, not a negative.

My second important value is Leadership, again, not something easily acceptable to many around me when I was growing up. It was better to be quiet in my culture, something I struggled with, especially identifying as female in the '50s and '60s. Speaking out as a leader when I was in a marriage was not acceptable either. I eventually accepted my leadership value as a strength rather than a challenge. For the last 30 years, I have led others by facilitating courses, helping others age with style into the person they want to be.

My third value for many years was Independence, but it is now Friends. Why? My handful of close friends are very important to me, especially the older I am. I make sure I check in with them at least once every two weeks no matter where I am living or traveling at the time.

Determining your values before you go any further is one of the most important things you can do for yourself. There are no right or wrong answers, but if you are living your parents' or your spouse's values, not yours, you may be unhappy or frustrated. If you are working in a job or career that doesn't allow you to maintain your basic values, you may be in the wrong profession. You can choose to live or work in the same place with someone while respecting each other's values, but there still must be commitment to communication.

A Story about Values
Years ago, I met a teenager through an organization where we were both volunteering. I was a young mother at the time. After getting to know him, I found out his dream was to become one of the best referees in the NHL (National Hockey League). He worked part-time to pay for skating lessons and volunteered with the local junior hockey team, and he was doing everything he could to make enough money to go to referee school when he graduated.

Looking back, I would say his values included personal motivation and being respectful to everyone around him. He was always well-dressed and clean, too. I mention that because I had to drop something off for him where he lived with his parents and younger sister, and he invited me in. There was garbage everywhere and narrow pathways led to other parts of the house past mounds of dirty clothes, stacked newspapers, and old takeout food containers. The kitchen counter was covered with dirty dishes, spoiled food, and what looked like rat droppings.

My young friend quickly led me through the chaos to his bedroom, a clean sanctuary, and offered me a chair to sit on. He didn't apologize for the mess his parents and sister lived in. I had so much respect for how he managed to not follow his family values. Somehow, he decided he wasn't going to live that way and did what he could to get out of that lifestyle, eventually leaving to begin a new life.

Reflecting on Values
Like I did above, decide what your three top values are. Then, determine how you live those values. It may take time to determine your values. An example: if you say tranquility is one of your three top values, but you yell every time someone cuts you off in traffic, maybe it isn't a value that you live by. Is it your value or the value of someone else? What can you do for yourself to resonate with the tranquility value?

Think of a person you admire. What do you like about that person? What turns you off about certain people or makes you angry when you are around them? Do they have traits or personalities that don't resonate with you even if they are part of your family or a leader in the community?

It can be helpful to google different lists of values to find the right ones for you.

CHAPTER 3: VALUES IN A LOVE RELATIONSHIP

I wrote the following as a stand-alone section on values. If you are entering a love relationship, try to determine your values before cohabiting, and then have a conversation with your prospective partner!

When I was writing this section, one of my readers pointed out that he wished he'd had this information about values before marrying, and, eventually, divorcing.

Straight people raised in the '50s or '60s were expected to marry before sleeping with each other (often not the case though) and having children, and then the wife would stay home to raise them. Divorce wasn't popular. Many grew up in that generation with the saying, "You made your bed, now lie in it!"

No matter why a marriage ended, divorce was a difficult process until the late '60s when Canada and the United States began introducing the no-fault divorce. But, mainly for women, there was a stigma attached to divorce. It was a struggle for women to have legal rights when it involved banking and establishing credit on their signature.

Fast forward a generation and North American values have changed drastically. Couples live together without marrying, and many choose not to have children. If they have children, both parents often work outside of the home. You may ask what has this to do with aging in style?

The older generation (often referred to as baby boomers) struggled with values different from the younger generation. The baby boomers were going to do what they could to keep a relationship together despite having different values from their spouse. Change began to happen over the decades.

According to research published in the *Journals of Gerontology* in September 2022, more than one in three people who divorce in the United States are now older than 50. That means that one in three divorcées were born before 1974. Whatever their values were around marriage earlier in life have changed over the years.

No matter what age a person is, their values can change. What they believed in and accepted earlier in life can change. The more people learn about themselves, the more they allow themselves to grow and move forward. Maybe your parents and your siblings won't understand, but changing your values is okay and part of how to age in style.

A Story about Values in a Love Relationship

I will share a personal story as it resonates with many people my age, and, for others, can hopefully help impart the impact shared (or differing) values have on a relationship. In my first marriage, my husband and I didn't think the same about many things. Our values were quite different, but I didn't begin to understand the effects of that on a relationship until I was long out of it. I remember a comment he made less than a year after we married while we were in the middle of an argument, "Why aren't you more like your mother?" I still giggle every time I think about that statement. The last person I wanted to be was my mother. Even though she was a nice person, she wasn't me! She was from an earlier generation who stayed home during my childhood, cooking dinner every night, year in and year out, and was never "allowed" to work outside the home.

There I was, growing up in the '60s, and, at 20 years old, I married a 22-year-old. Remember the cerebral cortex explanation in the introduction? I didn't ask my husband why he thought I should be like my mother. I had already determined I didn't want to be anything like her. I imagine my own daughter feels the same way!

Our marriage was rocky, but we were committed to making it work, just like our parents before us. Both of us were determined even though our values were changing and going in different directions.

We finally ended our marriage, almost 25 years in, after our two children were adults and we were empty nesters. I don't regret for a minute the experiences I had in those 25 years because I learned much about myself and knew who I didn't want to be! It took time for me to understand that though. It also took time for me to accept responsibility for the part I played in the marriage and subsequent breakdown.

I gradually learned what my values were and embraced them as a single person. When I entered a second relationship which also led to marriage three years later, I realized I still had many "marriage" values I had learned from my parents and my first marriage that I hadn't changed. The values that I connected to marriage or partnership weren't necessarily my values but ones "borrowed" from earlier generations. My second marriage ended, that time only five years in. Again, I learned more about who I was.

Reflecting on Values in a Love Relationship

Reflect on the following questions whether you are currently in a relationship or have been in one before and want to learn what you can do to make the next one better. These questions help you become more aware of the part you play in your relationship. You are never too old to learn something new about yourself. If you are uncomfortable digging into past relationships, take it as a sign that you have more work to do for yourself!

In your relationship, how do (or did you) resolve conflict? Do you sit down and communicate quietly with the other person? Do you yell? Do you refuse to discuss the conflict?

How has your partner learned to handle conflict?

What steps can you take to resolve conflict in your relationship?

How do you want your partner to support you in your relationship (emotionally, physically, monetarily)? How do you think you "should" support your partner? Is this your belief or your parents' belief?

Think about five things that you like about your partner or liked about your last partner.

Think about three things you don't like about them.

If you are currently in a relationship, ask for your partner's three top values. Compare your findings to see how they align or contrast. For example: Say family is one of your values. Do you go over and have dinner with your extended family every Sunday? What if you move away? How will it look then? What does it look like to your partner? If you have been in a relationship that has ended for any other reason than death, reflect on why it ended and what part you played in its ending. Do this for every relationship that has ended. Again, this is part of understanding yourself and your values. Until you understand who you are, you will struggle to move forward because you may keep repeating the same issues.

Please note: If you feel you are in any type of abusive relationship (physical or emotional) please seek help to protect yourself. Abuse can affect people of any age or gender, and there are many resources out there for you, both in-person and online. If you question whether you are in that type of relationship, whether the abuse is from your spouse, a family member, or your boss, what actions can you take to protect yourself?

CHAPTER 4: WHO WERE YOU?

*A*s you age, you often identify as what you do, not who you are. You connect with your career and your family roles, no matter how young or old you are. Who are you without those roles? How do you identify with the person inside of you? Sometimes the relationships you have with parents, a spouse, business partner, coworkers, or friends may keep you from really learning to embrace the person you would have, should have, could have been. I want to challenge you to look at yourself.

I don't know what you believe about yourself right now, but going through this process will open your eyes to new possibilities and new ways of thinking. I know where my journey has taken me, but how about you? Where have you been and where do you want to go from here? Do you want a new job, a new way of living, a new partner?

Before you read any further, there are some terms I would like you to think about. Many people are stuck in roles they learned as they grew up.

The following definitions, in part or in full, have been pulled from Oxford Languages.

- **Victim:** A person who has suffered at the hands of someone else or is in a situation that is out of their control.
- **Passive or Aggressive:** Passive means refusing to communicate because you might say the wrong thing. Aggressive means speaking forcefully and loudly without considering the feelings of others around you. A passive person may suddenly turn aggressive for many reasons, but it is often a learned response.
- **Assertive:** Being assertive shows respect for yourself and others. You stand up for your beliefs but are respectful to others while you express your thoughts and feelings. It isn't always easy to learn how to be assertive.

Remember, everything that has happened to you before this point has made you who you are today. It requires work on your part to get beyond your deep-seated beliefs. Negative messages you receive as a child from a parent, a teacher, and possibly later from a partner, affect the way you feel about yourself. Until you identify those negative messages, you won't be able to change them. Know that you can change direction at any age.

A Story about Who She Was
Lora was a woman about my age whom I met while taking a psychology course at college.

She was raised in a household during the '50s and '60s, where her parents expected her to eventually take a traditional role of housewife and mother when she left home. She learned to not talk back to her father even though she didn't necessarily agree with what he said. Nor did Lora talk back to her husband, so she didn't learn how to communicate in a relationship. She learned from her mother that if a woman spoke up in her marriage, she was being aggressive. Before having children, Lora worked as a secretary outside of the home and eventually became an executive secretary. In her position, she was responsible for many things and had no problem speaking assertively to her boss. When she spoke to her husband in the same manner, he accused her of being aggressive. She finally left work to have children.

Lora's marriage ended when her children were still young. She believed that the end of her relationship was all her husband's fault and that she hadn't caused anything to do with the marriage breakdown. Lora could choose to remain a victim, or she could choose to move beyond that way of thinking. She started dating again, but it took time for her to become more assertive and respect others even if she didn't agree with their opinions. Eventually, she learned to say "I don't know" when she didn't. She finally met someone with similar values who respected her and what she had to say.

Reflecting on Who You Were
Now that you have looked at your values, I have a question: "What else do you know about who you were?" Think about your earliest childhood memory and the reason you remember it. If you find there is still trauma attached as you think about your earlier years or where you are now, please follow up with a professional if you haven't done so already.

Do you feel you are a victim in your current relationship, job, or living situation? How do you react to conflict in different relationships, at home, at work, and with friends? Do you consider yourself a victim, passive, aggressive, or assertive? Is there a difference in your behavior in different settings? Why?

Add more stories as you remember other experiences in childhood/adolescence that made an impression on you and the way you thought. Realize that everything you have experienced and learned then is part of who you are now as an adult. These experiences will affect whether you think about yourself positively or negatively. The next few chapters will hopefully help you learn new ways of thinking.

CHAPTER 5: YOUR BRAVE SELF

*E*ven though it may be a difficult journey for you to look at things you have done in the past, you have all taken some sort of risk in your life.

I thought about all the times I thought I was brave as a child/teenager:

- Climbing on to a shed with a group of five-year-old boys and falling off the roof.
- Renting a rowboat by myself for my 11th birthday.
- Riding my bike 12 miles to visit my aunt when I was 12.
- Skipping school and going down to the city's East End by myself at 16.
- Traveling solo across Canada on a Greyhound bus after graduation at 17.

A Story about Bravery

This is a story about bravery from my own childhood, told from the perspective of 11-year-old me.

I came up with this great idea to celebrate my birthday a few months ago. I was almost 11 years old and feeling rich because I had started babysitting for 25¢ an hour at the age of 10. After becoming one of the top sitters in the neighborhood (or the only sitter), my money jar was full. I already felt good that I could buy gifts for special occasions for my family members, and now I decided I wanted to do something special for myself, too.

My plan was to rent a rowboat and take it out for three hours on Deer Lake on my birthday, a small lake close to where I lived. I had already checked with the boat rental operator to find out what it would cost.

The day of my birthday finally arrived, "Mom, I'm walking down to the lake," I said to her after breakfast. She knew it was something I did regularly in the summer.

I could feel my excitement building as I made my way down the street and to the top of the lake trail. I had my hand in my pocket, clutching the three dollars in quarters that it would cost me.

I soon reached the boatshed, and the boat rental operator didn't blink an eye even though he probably knew I was too young to be going out in the boat by myself. He took my money and handed me a set of oars. The only other experience I'd had in a rowboat was last year on the same lake in my dad's homebuilt ten-foot punt while participating in a children's catfish fishing derby.

The reason I wanted to row on Deer Lake was to see the front of Oakalla Prison which was located on the other side of the lake. Because we lived near the prison, my young imagination was fed by the alarms going off occasionally, announcing a prison break. We would see a man or woman dressed in gray prison garb run through a neighbor's yard, and the police would be notified.

What did the prison look like from the water? The closest I'd ever managed to get before was on foot through the bush. I had reached the high cement prison fence, topped by barbed wire, surrounding whatever was inside. I knew then that there must have been another way a prisoner could escape, and I wanted to check it out.

I put the ratty lifebelt that came with the rental around my waist. It was too big for me, but I had read enough books to know I could hold on to it to keep me afloat if I went overboard. I struggled to put the oars in the oarlocks because they were long and heavy, but, eventually, I managed to move the boat forward. I planned to take an hour to get across the lake and an hour to return. That would give me lots of time to look around.

My hands were sweaty with a combination of excitement and fear as I rowed. It only took me three-quarters of an hour to cross the lake to where I could see the front of the prison, so I was already well ahead of schedule.

The building that I saw located at the back of the property was old, built with weathered gray stone which looked cold even in the heat of the summer. I heard a sudden splash beside the boat and, thinking of escaped prisoners, felt my heart in my mouth! I couldn't see anything at first, looking over my shoulder at the noise. There was another splash, this time on the other side of the boat! My eyes watched the huge ripples make their way from the boat. I held my breath, waiting to see what would happen next.

Two beady eyes appeared, followed by whiskers. It was a huge catfish, bigger than any I had seen before. I breathed a sigh of relief because I had done what I planned to do on my adventure. I rowed my way back to the dock, glad I satisfied my curiosity.

Reflecting on Your Brave Self

Think about those risks you took, look at them more closely and realize how brave you were at an earlier time. Once you discover your time(s) as a risk-taker, it will open avenues for you to move forward. Look at yourself as a risk-taker, as a child and as a teen. Pick one brave thing from your list that still resonates with you. Then share the story with a friend or relative, child, grandchild, niece, or nephew. Learning to share your authentic self is an important part of your journey. How did you feel about sharing your story?

CHAPTER 6: YOUR FEARFUL SELF

*M*any children have read Mark Twain's novel, *The Adventures of Tom Sawyer*. One of the scenes in the book takes place in a cave, where Tom and his girlfriend, Becky, become lost and wander in the cave for several days. I can still recall the fear inside of me as I read that chapter, one reason being I had a very active imagination!

So often the fear within you is a result of experiences in childhood, and until you identify them and let them go, those fears are stopping you from moving forward. I'm sure all of you have been there at one time or another. Fear is something that can keep you from being your best person.

The following were fears I had:
- Fear of not being perfect (not being good enough)
- Fear of being too outspoken
- Fear of being too smart (yes, you read that right!)
- Fear of heights
- Fear of snakes
- Fear of deep water
- Fear of not being loved
- Fear of rejection
- Fear of failure
- Later in life—fear of being old

As you see, my fear list is much longer than my brave list, and I know from experience that others doing these sections will find the same. Dr. Susan Jeffers, an American psychologist, wrote the book *Feel the Fear and Do It Anyway* in 1987, and it became a bestseller, translated into 30-plus languages. The self-help book was based on her own life, making it more relatable for many readers.

As you move through this section, keep in mind that addressing your fears may trigger unresolved childhood trauma. If that is the case, please seek professional help to work through it.

A Story about Fear

My biggest fear when I first did this exercise was the fear of heights. I was only 10 years old when my fear of heights developed. We were going on a camping trip and stopped at a restaurant along the way which overlooked the river canyon. As my dad was parking, the car's brake slipped, and the driver's front wheel went over the edge. Mom screamed, so I screamed too because all we could see was the river below. It was a scary moment in time, but we all survived.

Years later, I made the mistake of telling a guy I was dating at the time about my cliff incident. We were parked at a local "lovers" point overlooking the city. When he started the car, he thought it was funny to let the car roll forward to the edge. I was soon screaming, and tears were running down my face.

Another situation happened years later when I was dating someone else whom I also told about my early childhood experience. We were standing on the cliff's edge of Bryce Canyon at the 10,000-foot level, looking down, when he grabbed me by the shoulders and pushed me closer to the edge. There was no guardrail and I screamed; once again, the tears were running freely. It took 25 years to work through my fear, through climbing heights that were out of my comfort zone. Even though it took me a year of "baby steps," I finally accomplished it.

Reflecting on Your Fears

This part of your journey is looking at your fears. What is stopping you from making changes? Hopefully, the following steps will help you move beyond your fears.

Everyone has fears, but remember, you are the only one who knows what is on your list unless you share. You may have one thing or many things that cause you fear. What are the fears that you have carried throughout your life and still carry, or ones you developed later in life? Think about all the fears you have and pick one that is always with you, that stops you from doing something outside of your comfort zone. Pick your top fear and tell yourself your story of how you ended up with that fear. Then, think about all the ways that you can let go of the fear you have.

CHAPTER 7: TRANSITION

The meaning of transition is complex, but simply, it's the process of changing from one state or condition to another. As we grow, relationships may change, and even end, with family, friends, and spouses. Later in life, new people enter and exit your life, and there is a good chance every person goes through these transitions. What steps do you want to take, possibly leaving others you have known behind because of the changes you make for yourself? You know where you have been, but where do you want to go from here? How to age in style is your choice!

What do you like about yourself? I know that may sound like a ridiculous question, but so often we think we think of ourselves as what we do, not who we are. We connect with our careers and our family roles, but who are we without those roles? When you are transitioning, whether you have come out of a long-term relationship, been laid off from your job, recently retired, or just want to change your lifestyle, sometimes it's difficult to define who you are now. Do you like who you are now?

One lady I knew struggled with this process when she came out of an extremely abusive relationship and was transitioning. She couldn't come up with one single thing she liked about herself at first. In her case, she had to start with something very small. She finally conceded that she liked her ears and how earrings looked on them. It was a beginning for her to open to the process of seeing herself positively. Hopefully, it won't be as difficult for you.

Maybe you've had the opportunity to do some human resources training at work, where you had to look closely at yourself. Even if you have, you can always learn more. As you read the next few paragraphs, reflect on how you have transitioned over the years.

Each person plays many roles, depending on age and circumstance. For instance, were you a teacher . . . teaching what? Boss/employee . . . what type of occupation? Certain themes will often be repeated at different times in your life. These are some of the roles people have played:

- Athlete
- Mentor
- Peacemaker
- Advocate
- Intellectual
- Writer
- Artist/musician

- Preacher/pastor/minister/priest
- Medical officer (doctor/nurse/paramedic/first aid attendant)

I wrote my list and had over 50 things on it. Please understand that I am almost three-fourths of a century old and have had many life experiences. It was also easy to determine the things I had done and experienced that I never wanted to repeat! I have transitioned many times during my life.

Stories about Transition

I am sharing stories about three people I know who also went through a transition, but I've not used their names to protect their privacy.

Person #1 had a very dysfunctional childhood with a mother who was unable to help her make good decisions and keep her safe from the mother's predator boyfriends. In fact, my friend became the mother in her household when she was still a child herself. She moved away from home as a teenager, found herself pregnant, and chose to raise her child. Less than two decades later she was a mother to three children, all with different fathers, and a grandmother to one. Even with a difficult start, she managed to go to university, receive a degree in education, and a master's in business. She made a difference to both children and adults, especially to her students. She moved to a different country when she was in her late 30s, built a small apartment building, and rented the units out as a means of income for herself. Her story could have been much different had she chosen not to follow her own path.

Person #2 is about the same age as I am and grew up in a small prairie town, went to university nearby, and eventually married a childhood friend. The pair moved to the big city, but a couple of years later, he began questioning his sexuality and soon realized he was more attracted to men than to his wife. He talked to his best friend at the time (his wife), and she was relieved as she had figured out that may be the case. They divorced and she eventually remarried. When he came out, he was lucky that his parents and other family members accepted him, a rare occurrence 50 years ago. He and his ex-wife remain good friends, and he still visits her and her husband occasionally. His story could have been much different, especially had he not had the support of family. Even then, it was his choice to live as himself.

I was a friend of person #3's grandmother, and I ended up renting a room in her daughter's house for a short time. My friend's daughter and granddaughter, who was a teenager at the time, also lived in the house with us, so I got to know both. I eventually moved away, but a few years later I ran into my friend again and found out she had just become a great grandmother to a set of twins. The other news was her granddaughter was now her grandson. Having a grandson was a shock to her at first, but she eventually understood her grandson's decision to physically transition as she spent more time with him post-transition. Having people who knew him pre-transition love him for who he is helped him become the person he wanted to be.

Thank goodness we live in a country where same-sex couples have protections and gender-affirming care is (albeit increasingly less) accessible, but that doesn't necessarily mean that the people closest to us will accept the changes we make as adults, or they may take time to accept who we are now. Just as it takes time for us to transition into the way we want to be, it also takes time for others around us to accept who we are becoming.

Transition can be huge and traumatic in a person's life and to all the people around them, or it can be easy with very little drama. It is important to be mindful of the person transitioning but also to those who are affected by the transition. There are so many stories that can be told about people changing their directions in life, transitioning to a new way of living. Change can occur early in life, or as people enter adulthood, or, in some cases, many decades later. Sometimes, the seeds for change were already planted early, and other times, change happens because of trauma that has occurred in a person's life somewhere along the way. Whatever the reason, it all comes down to the fact that every person deserves to be happy, regardless of what those around them think!

I consider myself lucky that I have met people from many different walks of life. I have witnessed the effects of racism and bigotry. I have learned to treat others with dignity and respect, maintaining the golden rule in my basic values: "Do unto others as you would have them do unto you."

With age also comes wisdom. Knowing what I won't tolerate from others and understanding when to walk away has been a very big part of my personal transition as I learn How to Age (in Style!).

Reflecting on Transition

Think about or write down at least five things you like about yourself (e.g., I'm nice, I'm a good friend, I'm a hard worker). If you struggle with this, ask a close friend for suggestions. Then think about the roles you have played in your life to date and what resonated the most with you? When you make your list, you may be as surprised as I was by the number of things you have done and the roles you have played. Mentally or on paper, check off those that were most important to you.

Using the same list again, mark things that you considered positive with a P, what you enjoyed the most, and what you were passionate about. For things that you didn't enjoy doing, that were negative, mark them with an N.

Revisit the things that you have listed as positive and negative. If the role was negative in a relationship with a spouse or parents, could it have been something positive outside the relationship? If that is the case, move it over to the positive list and put an asterisk beside it.

Finally, draw a line through those things that you would never repeat!

As you make your list, note again if you have taken on that role more than once. That is often where your strengths are. Often you don't recognize them until you see them on paper or reflect on them.

CHAPTER 8: DARE TO DREAM

So often you are caught up in everyone else's dreams that you don't take time to look at yours. Part of my moving on, as a newly single person, was permitting myself to dream, something I hadn't done in a very long time.

As you begin this process of dreaming, I want you to be in a positive state of mind. Think of one positive thing that you identified about yourself in the last chapter.

Start with a short meditation, shut your eyes, and dream! One of my dreams was returning to school, and I accomplished it, so I know it is possible. It doesn't matter what age you are; it is never too early or late to learn how to dream! First though, if you have only read through the material and not done any reflections, you may want to go back and do that now.

I'm sure you are aware of many motivational speakers like Tony Robbins, Brené Brown, Eckhart Tolle, and Oprah Winfrey. They encourage others to dream. This is only a small list of people who have made a difference in how others think. There are many musicians, sports personalities, and activists who have also encouraged others to dream. Martin Luther King, Jr., in his speech on August 28, 1963, "I Have a Dream," made a huge difference when he called for civil and economic rights and an end to racism in the United States.

The Stonewall Uprising in Greenwich Village, Manhattan, NYC in June 1969 was a landmark event which opened the door for the LGBTQ+ rights movement worldwide. The movement happened because a group of people had a dream.

I went down many fact-checking rabbit holes as I did research for this section. One of the facts I found was through the National Science Foundation, which was established as a federal agency in 1950 and, since then, has supported basic research driven by curiosity and discovery. According to the agency, as cited in *Psychology Today*, "An average person has about 12,000 to 60,000 thoughts per day. Of those, 80 percent are negative, and 95 percent are exactly the same repetitive thoughts as the day before and about 80 percent negative." Therefore, we think negatively much more than positively during the day. What has that to do with dreaming, you may ask? It makes it difficult to dream if you are inundated with negative thoughts each day.

Some examples of dreams are a new job, new partner, trip(s), education, healthy lifestyle, new car, personal "daredevil" challenge, etc. A dream I have is to go skydiving at the ripe old age of 85! I have decided to leave that dream until I reach that age because if something were to happen, a heart attack jumping out of the plane, or the chute not opening, I wouldn't be missing the next few years of realizing other dreams!

A Story about Dreaming

In the mid-1990s, I developed a weekend workshop for youth at risk called "Dare to Dream." The group of teens attending the workshop were 16 and 17 years old and had gone through the justice system. You can imagine how many negative thoughts inundated their daily lives! They didn't know one another but had chosen the workshop option to put in volunteer hours required by the court.

Introductions to one another was a challenge, and, of course, I was the enemy as the adult leader. I quickly determined that a couple of the teens seemed to have the ability to lead and asked them to coordinate an exercise to introduce one another using play, which they did.

Over the next few hours, I facilitated small and large group discussions, constantly changing the people in each group. By the end of the day, they knew a couple of things about all the other teens there.

Many of the teens taking the workshop were afraid to dream at first because of old messages. They might have had a teacher who told their parents, "Your child is a daydreamer!" which stopped so many children from dreaming. I too was told that when I was growing up, and it stopped me from dreaming for a while.

The most powerful exercise they did, though, was at the end of the first day. I passed out 12 sheets of paper with 12 names on each, the number of teens taking the workshop. I asked each teen to write one positive word on each person's sheet. If they couldn't think of anything positive to say about a certain person, they were to leave it blank. After they finished that exercise, I passed out blank cardstock and asked them to write one positive word about themselves and then decorate the card using supplies I'd brought with me. Before they headed to bed that night, I gave each of them their list of positive words, written by their colleagues. A couple of them had tears in their eyes after reading the list, and I will hazard a guess that it was the first time they had read positive words about themselves.

I share this story because the learning process they went through during the weekend made a difference in the way they thought about things. They did the same things as you are doing in this zine, discovering values, determining who they had been and who they are now, and learning how to dream. Some of the teens allowed themselves to dream for the first time in their lives. They realized we all have the right to dream!

Reflecting on Dreaming

Reflect on the things you have wanted to do or be in your life. It does not matter what age you are now or how crazy you think your ideas are. These are thoughts or ideas that may have crowded your brain for years, and now I am encouraging you to let them out. Before you begin, close your eyes, take a few deep breaths in and out, and relax. You can write words, short notes, or long sentences. If you don't want to write, you can make a mental list, but know that a written list will be helpful to have once you reach Chapter 17.

Hopefully, as you do this exercise, more dreams will continue to appear. You may be thinking, "Argh, this is going to be work!" Yes, but it helps you to go forward in your life, set goals to realize your dreams, and enjoy the rest of your life, living up to your potential! Overcoming my fear of heights was on my list of dreams, and I eventually set a goal to do it.

Remember, no idea is stupid, ridiculous, or crazy, even if you have been told otherwise! Your dreams can be as far-fetched as you want, and that is okay.

Up until now, I have asked you to reflect on each section, whether you write down your thoughts or not. This is a time that you may want to keep a physical record of your dreams, on your phone or in a notebook, so you can visualize those dreams even more. When you are ready, put your list of dreams where you will see it first thing every morning. Read it at least once a day! Add to the list, for at least two weeks, as more dreams come to mind. Make it colorful and visual, easily noticeable.

Ignore other people's advice because this is your dream list, not someone else's! Try not to share your ideas yet because you may end up with feedback you don't want to hear!

When you have compiled your list of dreams, note after each whether it is important for your mind (M), body (B), or spirit (S). Sometimes it is for all three. Finally, for the analyzers out there, make short notes about "why" you have each dream. Is it something you've always dreamed of accomplishing? Is it your dream, or a dream someone else had for you? Is it a fear you have had forever that you want to overcome? Remember, the notes you make are only for you.

CHAPTER 9: CHOICES

Oxford Languages defines "choice" as "an act of choosing between two or more possibilities."

This is the shortest chapter in the book but the most important when thinking about how to age in style. Everything you do in life requires you to make a choice. Sometimes your choices don't turn out the way you want because, deep in your subconsciousness, you are doing it for someone else, rather than for yourself. No matter how old you are, life is what you choose to make of it. Sometimes it means going in a new direction that you have never considered, especially if you are no longer where you want to be. At first, you may struggle with change and making choices, as I did, even when I knew it was the best thing for me. Could I be the person I wanted to be? Can you be the person you want to be?

As I was looking at my resource book list, I came across one that I hadn't read for many years, *The Road Less Traveled*, by M. Scott Peck, MD, I was surprised that it is still being read by the current generation, a book first published in 1978. To quote Dr. Peck, "Once we truly know that life is difficult—once we truly understand and accept it—then life is no longer difficult. Because once it is accepted, the fact that life is difficult no longer matters."

What I want to share is that making a choice is the difficult part. Once we have made that choice, it is no longer difficult.

A Story about Choices

You have choices and you are the only person who can make choices for yourself or keep those choices from happening. Every time you use the word "can't" you are making a choice! Every time you say "should" you are making a choice!

The following was shared by a friend. "When my son was young, I interrupted him every time he used the word 'should.' I said, 'Should is not a word we use in this house. You will do it, or you won't do it, you could do it, but you have a choice to do it or not.'"

It is your choice to learn new strategies, skills, tools . . . or not! It doesn't matter what others have told you while you were growing up. When you reach adulthood, whatever age you consider that to be, it is your choices that will determine what you are going to believe and how you will move forward to become the best person you can be!

Reflecting on Choices

What does a healthy lifestyle look like for you? What do you want to do on a daily, weekly, or yearly basis? Do you want to visit people, travel, earn a degree, or live a healthier lifestyle? Are you a smoker, drinker, gambler, or drug user, and if so, do any of those habits affect your quality of life or health? Again, look at your dreams and see what choices you want to make for yourself. I will discuss more about setting goals to realize your dreams in a later section.

CHAPTER 10: BOUNDARIES

Boundaries are the rules that you set for yourself in your relationships, whether it is a love, a friendship, or a working relationship. A personal boundary can be described as where your responsibility ends in a relationship and the other person's responsibility begins.

Dr. Brené Brown is well-known for her lessons and podcasts on the importance of knowing when and how to say no. To quote Dr. Brown in her special *The Call to Courage*, "We can't base our own worthiness on others' approval. Only when we believe deep down that we are enough, can we say 'enough.'"

If you are like many people, it is easy to stretch personal boundaries to the point where you give too much time to others and not enough time to yourself. Sometimes, even when there is a crisis, you must learn to look after yourself first. Setting boundaries is an important part of not only taking care of your mental health but also taking care of your physical and emotional health.

Think about the following scenario:

· · · · ·

"I am so tired because I end up doing a lot of things I don't want to do for others. Other people end up draining a lot of my energy and time."

"So, you enjoy giving away your energy and time?"

"I just like helping people."

"But you just told me you are drained because of what you have been giving out to others. Helping others is a win-win scenario, a positive experience, not a negative one."

· · · · ·

Learning to love ourselves is learning to know ourselves and our limits.

Another way to think about boundaries is in terms of self-care. Self-care is the ways in which a person acts to preserve one's own health and happiness. Boundaries *are* self-care. For me, the best thing I can do for myself is to walk or sit beside the water. Another thing I like doing is going for a relaxing massage, not just one that is therapeutic. When things are tough, I will often escape for a few days. I know my closest friends are there, and I have learned to reach out to them, if necessary, by phone or email. I also enjoy reading or listening to audio books.

Setting boundaries and self-care are among the most difficult things we learn to do for ourselves, especially women, as there is more chance that the person who identifies as female will be a caregiver because of learned generational messages.

I'm sure you realize by now how values and boundaries are interchangeable, and how it is necessary to understand what yours are. The last thing I will mention is it is important to listen to your intuition because it will help you determine your values and your boundaries so you can make the best choices for self-care. Remember, your self-care may look different from that of another person, so be aware of people in your life telling you how your self-care "should" look. There is that word again!

A Story about Boundaries

If you were a woman growing up in the '50s and '60s, there was a good chance that you learned to be a caregiver at a very young age. The expectations were that you would learn to do the "women's" work in your household, including helping to care for your siblings. That continued into your married life when you became the main caregiver, especially if you chose to have kids. Setting boundaries was not talked about. You were just there to carry out your expected "role."

Now that people are living longer, there is a good chance that the man in this type of straight relationship may become a caregiver for his wife as well.

I knew a couple who were both extremely intelligent professors at the university level. The woman began showing signs of dementia in her early '60s, and the disease progressed rapidly. Her husband took on the caregiver role, even though he was well able to afford outside care for her. As a result, he burned himself out, not taking time to do sports with friends, no longer socializing. His wife eventually had to go into full-time care, but it took him a few months before he was able to return to a normal life. Had he had boundaries in place and communicated with his wife before she was sick, they may have had a plan in place for this scenario.

Sometimes you will reach out to others because you think it will make you feel good about yourself and therefore the other person will feel good about you too. Often, these messages are ones you learned early in life. You may think helping others is one of your values, but if you feel you are giving too much of yourself all the time, then it is a learned value that isn't yours.

If it is your value, you can set boundaries for yourself. Without being able to set good personal boundaries and being able to say no, you can put yourself into an unhealthy desire to be everything to everyone. Please read this again! This behavior can cost you your physical, mental, and emotional health if you give away too much and don't practice self-care.

Reflecting on Boundaries

Reflection on your boundaries is one of the most difficult exercises throughout the process of aging in style, no matter your age or gender. Think about the following questions:

Do you feel you are giving too much of yourself away to others?

What is the name of the person taking your time? You might have to do this exercise for more than one person in your life.

What is the person asking of you?

What can you give of yourself to the person right now?

Are you offering help that you don't have time or energy to give?

Do you feel guilty for not doing more?

Do you have a hard time saying no?

If you are not there for the person, what will happen?

What do you want your self-care to look like when you set your boundaries?

Reflect on at least three things you currently do for self-care. If you currently don't do self-care, imagine three things you might enjoy doing, and add them to your list of dreams if they aren't on it already.

When you do something for yourself, how does that make you feel? Do you feel guilty/selfish, or do you feel you deserve it? When was the last time you practiced self-care? What does practicing self-care look like to you?

A strategy that is very effective in learning to set boundaries in a fun way, is to arrange with a friend to do a roleplay. Each one of you makes up a list of things you want the other person to do for/with you. You must have good reasons why you want the other person to do these things for you.

As you listen to each other's ideas, you will say no and continue to say no for as long as it takes for the other person to "hear" you. Setting your boundaries is about open and honest communication.

CHAPTER 11: DEVELOPING FRIENDSHIPS

riendships are one of the most important things you can do for yourself as you age. Sure, there are those kids you played with as a child and the "drinking/toking up" buddies you hung out with as a teen. Where are they now? Are they still around but grown up, or did you leave them behind as you grew up? Developing new friendships is not easy, no matter your age. Losing those social connections is one of the most difficult things you may face as you age. How can you make new friendships?

There were lots of years I chose to be a "loner," even when I was married, because I didn't trust myself to share who I was. I learned to speak up and share with others when I learned to ditch my comfort zone. That doesn't mean I share everything about myself with everyone. I have different levels of friendships because it takes time to build close relationships.

Let's look at the levels of life and friendships. There is your Public Life, which is that part you show to colleagues at a cocktail party or football game. Then there is your Private Life, which often includes your family, close friends, and spouse. These are the people you can count on for hugs, which is a huge part of friendship. Finally, there is your Secret Life, which is what you write in your daily journal or the information about you that is known only by one or two friends that you trust implicitly. It sometimes takes years to be able to share that part of who you are with another person, your fear of failure, your craziest moves, and your deepest thoughts. The person you share your deepest secrets with isn't necessarily your spouse either. It depends on how each of you communicate. Sometimes you don't want to share with your spouse, especially if you have been in more than one relationship over the years. The other option is to share your Secret Life only with a counselor.

The older you are, the more friends you begin to lose to illness and death, which is very difficult! Years ago, a 92-year-old friend told me the best thing I could do for myself is to make young friends. Most of his friends were at least 40 years younger than him, including me. I took his advice and have a few friends who are anywhere 10 to 30 years younger than me. I also have friends in both Canada and Mexico now because those are the two places I spend most of my time.

How do you build new friendships? Dr. Marisa G. Franco, a psychologist, and a professor at the University of Maryland, wrote the book Platonic: How the Science of Attachment Can Help You Make—and Keep—Friends. She addresses attachment styles and specific, research-based ways to improve friendships. Building friendships as an adult is much more complex than being a four-year-old child in a neighborhood saying "Hi" to the new kid on the block, or is it?

It takes work to develop a friendship that is two-sided. How much time are you willing to give to a friendship? How much time is that new friend willing to give to you? Many so-called friendships (not friends) end up very one-sided. It may be because one person is a giver and the other is a taker. Or one person is unable to trust anyone, which has nothing to do with the other person. Having an open mind and a positive attitude goes a long way when building a friendship. Try to become an active listener.

You have already read about choices, one of which includes the word "should." If you want to build a friendship, try to drop the word from your vocabulary. Don't use phrases like, "You shouldn't feel that way," or "You should do this." I never realized that I had the habit of using the "should" word until my youngest sister pointed it out to me years ago and told me that it made her feel stupid and unable to make her own decisions. She was right! It was a habit I learned growing up because my mother used it all the time when she was speaking to me. When I had it pointed out, I had to choose whether I would quit using the word, which I did, but it wasn't easy. I asked two friends, my sister, and my spouse to tell me every time I used it, and I was shocked at how often I said it! It took me about a month to break the habit!

Some people are never able to move beyond a surface friendship and build a relationship because of the stuff buried deep inside them. When you first meet someone new, that person may appear very open and share everything because there is no commitment at that point. How are they a few months later when you want them to become part of your Private Life? Are they willing to work on the friendship between the two of you? This is so important, especially if there is a possibility the friendship could develop into a love relationship later.

A Story about Building Friendships

When I moved to a place I'd never lived in before, I would go out for coffee once a week and strike up a conversation with a stranger, which was way out of my comfort zone since I consider myself an introvert. I realized the worst-case scenario is they would think I was crazy, but I ended up with a longtime friend that way with whom I'm still in touch! I had the opportunity to take a job in Mexico for a year, so when I had settled in, I made a list of what I liked doing, and then I looked for a group of people who liked doing the same things. I joined a writer's group, and out of the 50 people I met in that group, two are still friends 15 years later. I've also made great friends attending or facilitating courses and workshops because we were like-minded people. I've kept in touch with people I've worked with in other places too. Even though I've been retired for a long time, I still connect with them occasionally for a coffee or lunch.

Reflecting on Friendships

Think about who you have in your life now and whether they are part of your Public, Private, or Secret Life. How do you maintain each friendship?

Who is already in your friend circle? Are they positive people who are there to build you up when you need support, or are they pessimists who put down your thoughts and ideas? If you could choose new friends, what would they be like?

If you have lost that person who was closest to you, what are you going to do to replace that connection?

CHAPTER 12: INTIMACY AND SEX

*U*nless you are an intimacy specialist/therapist and/or have a partner who is very open to communicating about sex, you are probably much the same as many of us, struggling with what intimacy and sex is all about, whatever your age. It doesn't matter if you identify as straight or LGBTQ+. Understanding intimacy and sex and the part they play in your life is difficult and it may change as you age, even if you are still young in your thinking. They may not even show up at all, or very minimally for those who identify as asexual and/or aromantic. Let's revisit values again and take a closer look at what you think intimacy and sex represent in a relationship. The following questions may give you a clue as to how open you are when it comes to talking about sexuality.

How often do you think sex "should" happen in a relationship? Once a day, once a week, once a month?

Do you think you have to "work" on your sexual relationship? Why or why not?

What does the word "commitment" mean to you in a relationship when it comes to intimacy and sex?

What makes you uncomfortable when you talk about intimacy and sex with your partner? (Do you think you will be judged?)

Is it uncomfortable even reading these questions, and if so, why?

Do you think there is a difference between having sex and making love? If yes, what do you think is the difference?

If your culture has a strong religious background, do you think that what you have learned through your religion affects the way you think about intimacy and sex? If so, in what way?

I can't answer any of these questions for you. Only you and a potential partner can discuss the questions I've written above. It is so important to learn to love yourself first as an adult and not expect another person to have all the answers.

Dr. Cheryl Fraser, a well-known Canadian sex therapist, mentions in her video talks that many relationships end because one or both people involved aren't open to communicating about sex and intimacy. As you age, there are several issues that can occur for people of any gender, causing sexual disfunction. She mentions that it is more normal than people may realize . . .

whatever the age, sexual disfunction can be worked through if people are willing to communicate!

I also decided to add a section on dating because it may eventually lead to intimacy and sex. The opportunity to meet new people through friends and family is not as easy as it used to be. Meeting them in a neighborhood bar or pub isn't as safe as it was years ago. The key word there is neighborhood. How many of you know the people who live in your neighborhood anymore, or even in your apartment or condo building?

Many people have turned to online dating to meet people, but it isn't an easy process. The only advice I have to offer, having done online dating in my later life, is it is a good way to meet people if you take it to the next level immediately. What I mean by that is if you are interested in the person, arrange to meet within a week after connecting with them online, if possible. If they live nearby and aren't willing to do that, go on to the next person. If they live out of town, it may take more time but shouldn't take too much longer. Also, both of you must be prepared to travel to see each other. That way, you learn more about the other's surroundings.

The idea is to develop a friendship first, not go full force into a sexual relationship, unless that is all you want. Be honest with yourself and the person you meet. Talk about your values and listen to theirs and watch for the red flags. Here are some things to consider:

Are they married or in a long-term relationship?

What went wrong in their last relationship, and why did it end? If they don't want to talk about it, consider that a red flag. Remember, it takes two to make or break a relationship, and if you visit these questions right away, you will have a better idea of how the person communicates.

How much time do they have available to develop a relationship?

Do they have friends, and do they want to introduce their friends to you?

Do they have children and if so, what kind of relationship do they have with their kids?

How much do you know about that new person in your life? Has there been time to talk about values or dreams or fears? There is a good chance there is sexual energy happening with the new person you just met, but you don't have to act on it the first night! So many people get caught in a relationship that starts with sex that never has the time to develop into a friendship first. If that is all you are looking for, that is fine, but if you're not, it is easy to expend time and energy on a relationship that will end quickly because it was based on sex, not friendship.

As you explore the world of online dating, an important thing to be aware of is that there are many scammers looking to fund their various schemes and will prey on the lonely. If things feel too good to be true, if the person keeps making excuses as to why they can't meet up, and especially if they begin to ask for money, even if it's to travel to see you, these are red flags, and the person is likely involved with you for the wrong reasons.

A Story about Intimacy and Sex

I grew up before computers and recall being handed a book called *Health, Sex, and Birth Control* by my very embarrassed mother. Some of my friends didn't even get that much information. Unfortunately, sex education hasn't changed all that much over the decades in some cultures because beliefs around sex are still tied closely to religion, or it has been a taboo topic right up there with politics. I am not here to debate those beliefs. Communication about sex is still not as open as it could be, especially within the older generations. We each have our own stories to share. Know what yours looks like before becoming involved with someone new.

Did you grow up learning sex is something you shouldn't have to communicate about; it should just happen? That early value may interfere with creating a new relationship if one of you is threatened by talking about intimacy and sex.

Reflecting on Intimacy and Sex

In the 21st century, we are inundated with information on sex and intimacy through various forms of media. This may give you unrealistic ideas of what sex is all about, especially as you grow older, whether you are in a relationship or not. What have you learned about sex from watching TV or following social media? Do you feel it affects your communication with a partner or potential partner about how sex and lovemaking "should" look? Can you talk about sex and lovemaking with close friends, or is that taboo in your world?

CHAPTER 13: LIMITING BELIEFS

A limiting belief is a state of mind or belief about yourself that stops or restricts you from growing because you believe it to be the truth. Limiting beliefs are often messages left over from childhood, things that you believe about yourself because they're what an influential adult told you. Limiting beliefs can also be messages from other adults when you are in a relationship. It is necessary to identify your limiting beliefs and let them go before you can grow.

The following are examples of limiting beliefs:
- I have no talent.
- I'm too old.
- I'm not smart enough.
- I don't have enough money.
- I don't have a degree.

Dr. Joe Dispenza wrote a book, one of many, called *Breaking the Habit of Being Yourself: How to Lose Your Mind and Create a New One*. In his book, he explains that a person is not doomed by their genes, nor are they hardwired to be a certain way for the rest of their life.

If we look at our limiting beliefs and choose to change them, we can create our new reality.

Limiting beliefs are beliefs we have picked up from those around us, whether it is family, friends, or even strangers. We can learn to let them go by rewriting them into a positive form. This may be uncomfortable at first, but as you work through each limiting belief it will become easier. For example, "I'm not smart" in positive form becomes "I am smart." You may not believe it at first, but if that is the message you begin telling yourself again and again, you will eventually accept it because your brain starts believing it. One of the hardest steps to take is shifting negative limiting beliefs to positive beliefs. Start doing this regularly until it becomes a habit. You now have a strategy to turn negative thoughts into positive thoughts, but how do you ditch the negative energy that no longer serves you? How do you ditch the negative people in your life? We will address that in the next chapter.

A Story about Limiting Beliefs
I wanted to be a published writer, but I didn't have a college degree. I learned very early in life that I was stupid. Of course, I know now that I'm not, but that is a message I started with. My mother knew my grade-one teacher personally and told her to punish me as needed. Within the first week of grade one, I was told to sit on a stool facing the blackboard and given a dunce cap to wear. I was embarrassed and humiliated, and that stuck with me for years. In high school, my English teacher told me I had to get a degree if I wanted to publish, even though he thought I was a good writer. It would take me years to take a chance and submit my first piece of writing because I never felt smart enough. That was, until I learned new tools and understood my limiting beliefs.

Reflecting on Limiting Beliefs
Limiting beliefs come from a place of fear that you have carried from the past. Think about and try to identify your limiting beliefs, all the things that you have thought about doing as a profession, as a sport, as a hobby, etc. Then make a list of what stopped you.

CHAPTER 14: FORGIVENESS

I briefly touched on letting negative people go from your life in the last section, as well as in the section on choices. What if the person who is still causing you grief has been out of your life for years, or has passed away? The idea of forgiveness for many people is unimaginable, especially if there was abuse, but what if I told you that not forgiving that person only affects you? Not being able to forgive can keep a person locked in anger, even hate, for decades, even when that other person is long dead. What they often don't realize is it affects everyone around them. I am not saying you must forget what happened, but that holding on to the "hate" that goes with the memory won't allow you to move on.

So, how can you forgive? Developing healthy coping skills is one of the tools you can use. Here are some of them:

- Every time a negative memory comes to the surface, say to yourself, "I'm not feeling good right now. What is bothering me?"
- Take time to do a short meditation, and then think about the negative thoughts you have about that person.
- Talk to yourself about what is happening in your mind.
- Do something physical for yourself like walk or run the negative energy off.
- Write a letter or email to that person who you have allowed to stay in your head and feed you negative thoughts. You don't have to send the letter unless you want to. Knowing that you've said what you needed to say to that person or people is often enough to release the negative thoughts from your mind.

It is okay if you require some help from a professional along the way.

Forgiving doesn't necessarily happen overnight. Often, it is a process, but every time you hear that voice inside you saying, "I am not feeling good right now. What is bothering me?" and that person comes to mind, you have the strategy in place that you can follow. Allow yourself to forgive, not only that person but also yourself. Tell yourself you are sorry for what happened and that you love yourself: "I'm sorry. Please forgive me. I love myself. I loved you."

A Story about Forgiveness

My godmother's daughter (a friend of mine) was getting married in a few months. The bride-to-be asked her mother and her stepfather to attend her wedding.

"Is your father going to be there?" her mother asked.

"Of course," the bride-to-be replied. "He's giving me away."

"Then I won't be coming." Her mother had been divorced for 30-plus years, and both her and her ex-husband had remarried a long time before. She was unable to forgive and therefore refused to attend her only daughter's wedding, which was so sad. Even though it was very hurtful to the bride, she chose to stay in touch with her mother. They never talked about her mother not attending her wedding again because she knew it would turn into an argument that wouldn't end. The daughter felt rejected by her mother, but instead of holding on to those feelings, she took care of herself and worked through forgiveness for her mother with a therapist.

Reflecting on Forgiveness

Be aware of those people in your life, past or present, that you are unable to forgive. Why is it important for you to hold on to that memory that keeps you locked in sadness and even hate? What do you get from it? Think about what you can do to let the memory go. It doesn't mean the memory still won't come to mind occasionally, but it won't have the same intensity or power over you any longer. It is from the past and only exists in your mind, but there may be certain buttons pushed when you hold on to the memories. The person can't hurt you again unless you allow them to do so with your thoughts.

Keep in mind that traumatic events need to be dealt with, often with a therapist. If you shove them into a corner of your mind, they will often affect you negatively when you least expect it.

CHAPTER 15: POSITIVE THINKING

*P*racticing positive thinking means you approach unpleasantness more positively and productively. You think the best is going to happen, not the worst. How many of you grew up with negative people surrounding you, telling you that "the world is going to hell in a handbasket," to "wipe that silly grin off your face," and that "the glass is half empty?" Messages that you receive growing up set the stage for what you choose to believe. Is that what you want to believe? What choices can you make for yourself to change that way of thinking? Positive thinking is all about choice.

How can you think positively daily, especially if your world, and the whole world, is tumbling down around you?

Give yourself time, five minutes each morning, as you are waking up, to reflect on what you are grateful for today. It may be as simple as the fact you woke up or you are feeling healthy today, or you can still see without glasses, especially the older you are! You can always find something to be grateful for, but if you start the day with a negative thought, what do you think that does to your mindset? Life is too short to think negatively, but if that is how you currently think each morning as you wake up, what can you do to change that?

Verbalize what you are grateful for each morning, even if it's only one thing. Use "I language" to take ownership of your gratitude. "I feel grateful for . . ." Remember the woman who could only find one thing about herself to feel good about, to be grateful for, the way her ears looked wearing earrings? She was finally able to expand her "gratitudes."

Once you've mastered that, tell others what you are grateful for. This is more difficult at first and takes practice, but try to tell one person in your life, a spouse, a relative, a friend, or a colleague what you are grateful for each day. If you begin with one thing, it will eventually become a habit.

A Story about Positive Thinking

One of the most popular self-help books ever written was *The 7 Habits of Highly Effective People*, by Stephen Covey. One of the habits he recommended was to write your personal mission statement. Being able to refer to your personal mission statement in difficult times will help you with positive thinking. On the same subject, William Arruda and Deb Dib, authors of *Ditch. Dare. Do!: 66 Ways to Become Influential, Indispensable, and Incredibly Happy at Work*, share the following, "A personal mission statement is a critical piece of your brand because it helps you stay focused. We all have superpowers—things we do better than someone else. As we get older, we have more life experiences and acquire new skills. If your mission statement doesn't change, you risk not being relevant anymore."

I wrote my first personal mission statement 30 years ago in 1994, and I revisit it and revise it each year. My Mission Statement for 2024 is:

• • • • •

I will make a difference by complimenting someone today.

I will say one thing that I am grateful for today.

I will count the times I smile today.

I will do something special for myself once a month this year.

I will travel someplace new twice this year.

Reflecting on Positive Thinking

To help yourself with positive thinking, create a personal mission statement for yourself that explains who you are, how you think, and where you are going in one or two sentences. Your personal mission statement should motivate, challenge, and inspire you. It will communicate your vision and values and address their roles in your life. Many organizations write mission statements as a working part of their business. Everything they do refers to their mission statement. Do the same for yourself!

Think about the following:

- What are the three most important values in your life?
- How do you live those values?
- What are you most passionate about?
- How do you carry out your passion?
- What is your "superpower", part of your personality that shines through to others? This reflection may require asking someone who knows you well as we sometimes don't realize what a special gift we are to others.

CHAPTER 16: THE ART OF PLAY

When was the last time you laughed from the bottom of your belly? When was the last time you experienced laughter as you did as a child? A study by Toshitaka Morishima et. al titled "Effects of Laughter Therapy on Quality of Life in Patients with Cancer," has found how beneficial laughter therapy is to the treatment of cancer patients. Many in the medical system now recommend watching funny movies and sitcoms throughout the treatment process. The effects of a good laugh can last for forty-five minutes. Can you think back to a time when you laughed so hard you peed your pants? I can. I was playing the game spoons with a group of people. It's a memory I keep in a corner of my brain to pull out whenever I need it! As a child growing up, you laughed on average one hundred times a day. How many times a day do you laugh now? In a HelpGuide.org article, "The Benefits of Laughter," Lawrence Robinson, Melinda Smith, MA, and Jeanne Segal, PhD write, "Laughter strengthens your immune system, boosts mood, diminishes pain, and protects you from the damaging effects of stress."

Play is another thing that is especially important as you learn how to age in style. Show your children, grandchildren, or nephews and nieces how to fish or play ball or take them on outings that you enjoyed as a child. I take my granddaughter on public transit whenever I visit her, something she doesn't do with her parents. Play by sharing your plans and dreams with close friends.

I know it is never too late to follow your dreams because it has not stopped me, but many people reach an age where they quit growing, or is it that they quit dreaming and playing? It may be what they consider midlife, retirement, or later life. Some people even quit dreaming and playing in their twenties because of all the old messages they were given to believe!

I was talking to the person beside me on a plane recently and explained what I was writing about and how we often look at aging. He said that his father told him to "get all his dumb moves out of his system in his early twenties because by the time he was thirty he was expected to be a mature man."

I know I believed all of that at first, too, but now I believe that if you want to start dreaming again, to start imagining your perfect life, you must learn how to laugh and play again! If you want to design your happiest life, imagine being happy! Part of how to age in style is returning to that mindset of a simpler life where you smiled and laughed and spent time playing.

Learning to smile again and trust myself was just the beginning for me. Figuring out who I wanted to be and giving myself permission to dream was my most difficult transition.

I named this section "The Art of Play" because if you decide you want to start dreaming again, you are going to have to learn how to play again!

A Story about the Art of Play

Dr. Stuart Brown spent his career studying play. In his book *Play: How It Shapes the Brain, Opens the Imagination, and Invigorates the Soul* he writes about aging, "At some point we get older, however, we are made to feel guilty for playing. We are told it is unproductive, a waste of time, even sinful. The play that remains is, like league sports, mostly very organized, rigid, and competitive. We strive always to be productive, and if an activity doesn't teach us a skill, make us money, or get on the boss's good side, then we feel like we should not be doing it. Sometimes the sheer demands of daily living seem to rob us of the ability to play."

Years ago, when my son was still a teenager, I gave him heck for not working as hard as he could on his homework and getting the marks in his subjects I knew he was capable of achieving. His reply has always stuck with me, "Ma, I will only be this age once. Let me be a kid and play." I am very lucky because both my adult "kids" still know how to play!

Reflecting on Play

I realized how important this part of the journey was when I volunteered to develop and facilitate the weekend program for youth at risk that I referred to earlier in the zine. Those teens had lost hope, didn't believe in themselves, and had also lost the ability to play! They had to be careful about anything they did because it might be construed as something wrong. During the workshop I taught them how to meditate and took them on a journey in a spaceship in their mind. *Star Wars* music helped them set the scene, and they shared the experiences they were having. We talked about those experiences after the meditation ended, and they shared how much fun it was. I explained that they could use that tool anytime they needed it and play in this world or another. I explained how the process would look.

Shut your eyes, breathe deeply at least three times, in through the nose and out through the mouth. Keeping your eyes closed, imagine you have the opportunity to go to space, something you have never experienced. You are an adventurer, and you choose the role you want to be (e.g., a pilot). How does the role you are playing make you feel?

Using your five senses, what are you experiencing? What are you most excited about in your journey?

Now try this for yourself: think of something you've never experienced and allow your mind to wander in exploration. Consider playing relevant music or including a scent to help you on your journey.

When it is time to return to Earth, breathe deeply again and slowly open your eyes.

What made you smile about that journey?

CHAPTER 17: SETTING INTENTIONS AND MANIFESTING THEM

*A*n intention is a mental state in which a person commits themselves to a course of action or goal. The first time I heard about this process of setting an intention and then manifesting it was through a documentary film in 2006 called *The Secret* by Rhonda Byrne. I followed the advice given in the documentary for setting intentions. According to *Merriam-Webster*, an Intender is one who intends, by having in mind a purpose or a goal; to design for a specified use or future.

First, how does one turn a goal into an intention? It's necessary to focus your attention on the present. Even though my intention was for the future, I had to believe that it was already happening for me right now. I have listed steps I follow when I set my intention:

1. Be very clear and specific about what you want to happen.
2. Look at why you want that intention to happen right now, and list all the reasons you can think of.
3. Imagine what it would feel like if you were already living your intention. What can you do right now to be in the moment? Remember we talked about daydreaming, which is something you learned to do as a child before the adults around you discouraged it? A big part of this is learning to daydream again! This will help you realize the obstacles that may get in your way as you think through each step.
4. Part of setting your intention is how you first write it down and then verbalize it. For instance, say your intention is to spend a month in Bora Bora. Saying "I want to spend a month in Bora Bora" isn't going to get you there. Why? "I want" is a negative phrase because it is only a hope on your part. Try saying instead, "I am sitting on the beach in Bora Bora everyday and loving it!" You are already imagining it. See the difference? Be positive with every word you write and speak.
5. Trust that the universe will give you what you desire and ask for.

A Story about Setting Intentions and Manifesting Them

I worked as an English teacher in Puerto Vallarta in 2002 and loved it, but it was only a three-month position. I decided that I wanted to return to work in Mexico for a year, so on January 1, 2007, I wrote my intention, and posted it where I saw it daily. I also told close friends about my intention.

On April 1, 2007, I woke up and had a strong feeling that I was to check Craigslist for jobs in Puerto Vallarta. There was a posting for a teaching position beginning in August, so I immediately sent an email with my résumé attached. I received a reply the next day asking me when I was available for an online interview. An hour later, I received another email from a young woman who had worked with me between 2002 and 2004. I hadn't been in touch with her since I'd left that position, but I was being interviewed to replace her in Mexico. Everything fell into place, and I applied for a sabbatical from my then current job, and a few months later, I was on my way to Mexico! I had just turned 58-years-old.

In November 2006, Rhonda Byrne released her book called *The Secret*, which was based on the documentary. I took the book with me. While I was in Mexico, I set more intentions that also manifested, and I joined an Intenders group made up of international participants. When I returned to my home country a year later, I started an Intenders group there.

Reflecting on Intending and Manifesting

We discussed strategies that you can use to determine your dreams in Chapter 8. The next thing to do is to turn each dream into a goal. I want you to prioritize your list from Chapter 8 to no more than 10. Gradually, go through them and draw a line through the ones that are the *least* important *at this time*. Also, remove any that involve others directly. An example of this is "I plan to go to Ecuador with Joanne by the end of this year." Unless your real goal is to go to Ecuador by yourself, even if Joanne can't make it, take it off your list. The next step is to short-list your dreams to five. I know it may sound ridiculous, but this is another heart-wrenching move and one of the hardest steps to take! Suddenly you are crossing off five of your ten top dreams! It is difficult at first, but as you go through the process, you realize what is most important for you to accomplish now. I will mention that some people may have only come up with five dreams in total, and that is okay! Your crossing off will go a lot faster!

Renumber your list again. For instance, say you originally set your top dream as "I am going to lose fifteen pounds in the next six months." You have gone through the steps in this process and what you thought was your top dream at one time isn't even in your top five! Maybe traveling somewhere for a holiday is more important right now, and you need to concentrate on that first. This is about becoming a healthier and happier you and learning how to age in style. You are the only one who can determine your dreams and then turn your dreams into goals. When you have figured out your top five dreams, the next step is to determine your most important one. I use a special question to determine what my most important dream is:

"What if I suddenly find out that I only have six months left to live?" For me, a condition of this question is that I will be physically and mentally healthy during those six months and can do anything I want to do.

The next part is to manifest your intention. It takes very little work on your part once you learn the secret of how to do it!

CHAPTER 18: SOME FINAL THOUGHTS FOR THOSE OVER 70!

*I*didn't begin to feel old until I turned 70. Suddenly, I was dealing with things like brain fog, body changes, and anxiety. When I look back on that time, the world was right in the middle of COVID, and I think I blamed a lot on that, but the changes occur yearly now compared to every five years. For instance, I don't have the stamina for doing long drives that I used to have. So far, no one has complained about my driving. Will that happen? I don't know, but if it does, I hope I will have the opportunity to take a road test with a professional. The last thing I want is to be a menace on the road, and there are other options for transportation. If I can still walk, take the bus, or grab a taxi, I'm happy! What happens when walking becomes a real issue though? What will that look like?

What are your biggest fears about aging? Dementia, Alzheimer's, mobility, and dying are high on the list for many people. One of the things that must be dealt with as people age is the breakdown of their parts. Some of us will have been living with a number of these disabilities from a young age. For those of us that have been able-bodied, some of that is a result of nonaction that has occurred for years. Knees and hips are two (or four) of the most common replacement body parts for aging people.

The eyes aren't as clear as they used to be either, so next on the list is new glasses or cataract surgery. Then there is a person's hearing! My hearing was great until it wasn't! I realized that many of my friends were beginning to mumble. I remembered listening to my parents yell, not hearing one another, blaming each other for not listening. If that sounds like you or your partner, maybe it's time to get your hearing tested!

What if you began challenging your doctors about their beliefs on aging? If you are treated like you are an invisible old person when you see your medical specialist, is that what you will start to believe? Is the feedback you get negative or positive? It requires some self-advocacy to help your doctor understand that you aren't an old, doddering fool. You take care of your car and make sure it is always running well. If it isn't, you take it to your mechanic and get it fixed.

If your doctor tells you that your parts are getting old and worn out, do you ask how the doctor is going to fix you? If so, what answer do you get?

Another thing we can experience more as we age is boredom. One of my granddaughter's favorite expressions at the age of 10 was, "I'm bored!" We all know that the child, given a few minutes to think, will take themself out of that mindset and find something new.

Someone who is in their later years, however, might struggle with this a bit more. The older a person is, the more likely they are to get into a rut in their everyday living. They develop a routine that is the same, day in and day out. I realized I was reaching that point a few years ago as I approached retirement, so I changed paths and found something new that I was passionate about. In 2011, I wrote a 120-hour TESOL (Teaching English to Speakers of Other Languages) Certificate Course and began teaching it in my country and then took it to Mexico. I was 66 years old. I also set a goal to write my memoirs in the year I turned 70. Even though it took me a whole year, I accomplished my goal. At the age of 72, I developed and began facilitating my newest workshop, "Ditching Your Comfort Zone," designed for people 50 and over.

Older people who grew up in the '60s are also looking at different housing options as they age. The idea of cohabiting—sharing living space with other like-minded people—is making a comeback which will add to more socializing.

Each culture has certain sets of expectations and assumptions (stereotypes) about aging, all of which is part of socialization.

The biggest thing about aging is communication. The opportunity to share stories, ideas, and understanding between young and old in a caring environment is what will make the difference going forward in our world.

With this in mind, think about writing your eulogy. This may be an uncomfortable topic for many, but it is something I had the opportunity to do 30 years ago during a college course I was taking. When you finally die, which is inevitable, what do you want people to say about you at your celebration of life, wake, or whatever you want to call it? How have you lived your life to date, and what do you want to be said at the end of it? Write down words that you want people to remember you by. Thank you to my professor, Michael, for sharing this lesson many years ago. I realized the words I wrote set the plan for the way I would live the rest of my life.

There are so many ways you can learn how to age in style, including taking up new hobbies, resurrecting old ones, or even finding a new passion. Keep moving while researching ideas, even if you use assistance like a wheelchair, scooter, or cane. Go to dances, and if you aren't participating yourself, listen to the music, move your feet, and socialize. Go to the theater or out for dinner with friends.

Check out your wardrobe, and if it looks dowdy, get a few new (or new-to-you) clothes. You don't have to pay a fortune for clothes. Between sales, online purchases, and recycling in thrift stores, it is easy to upgrade your wardrobe to feel good about yourself. Ditch the frumpy clothes in your closet, and donate them immediately so you aren't tempted to wear them again. If you don't know how to begin finding style, take someone with fashion sense shopping with you. Think about a new hairstyle while you are at it, or if you have very little hair left, consider going bald.

Laugh a lot more. That will keep you looking and feeling younger quicker than anything.

Dr. David Lee, from the University of Manchester and NatCen Social Research, lead authored a paper titled "Sexual Health and Wellbeing among Older Men and Women in England" which determined people in their 70s and 80s continue to enjoy active sex lives. More than 7,000 people responded to the questionnaire, and more than half (54 percent) of men and almost a third (31 percent) of women over the age of 70 were still sexually active. It was the first study to also include people over 80. A third of both the sexually active men and women had frequent sex, meaning at least twice a month.

Even though we are in the 21st century, people over 70 are hesitant to talk about intimacy and sex. I believe much of that is a result of beliefs from the '50s and '60s when sex was still taboo in public and was still attached to procreation rather than enjoyment. Erectile dysfunction and vaginal dryness are physical issues that should not affect the ability for a couple to enjoy a fully satisfying love life no matter how old they are. Communication and learning more about sex and intimacy, even after 70, will improve the love life of the older baby boomer generation. It's foreplay (that word "play" again) that makes life good!

A Story for Those Over 70

"Social media in my day meant going next door to visit my neighbor or going to the local coffee shop." Have you heard an old geezer tell you that lately? Get over it, old people. Social media is here to stay, and it is wonderful! The first time I lived in a foreign country by myself was in 2002 at the age of 53. There were already internet cafés available, and it was my way of staying in touch with my kids who would then relay messages to my parents.

My granddaughter doesn't know a world without social media. More people are digital nomads since COVID, living and working all over the world. Don't forget about Siri or Alexa or the Google Maps lady! You can learn lots from them. The world is changing quickly, and AI (Artificial Intelligence) is here to stay and so much fun to play with! How is the world going to look in a few more years? Do you want to get left behind?

Final Reflections for Those Over 70

Even though you are getting older, realize that you can do something about its effects. It may be uncomfortable at first because it requires you to change and ditch your comfort zone, but it's well worth the investment. Make a list of what needs to be fixed (glasses, knee replacement, dental work, etc.) and figure out how you are going to fix what's broken.

Make one list of how savvy you already are when it comes to computers and technology and then another of what you still want to learn. Then do it!

We have many distinct cultures between the ages of twenty and ninety, and we need to learn from one another. For instance, many cultures are very uncomfortable around aging, dying, and death. What are your experiences and beliefs? If you believe you "should" be old at a certain age, you will be! Take some time to make a list of the stereotypes you have learned and still believe when it comes to aging.

ABOUT THE AUTHOR

Susan Gerle facilitates workshops/retreats a few times a year called "How to Age in Style by Expanding Your Comfort Zone" based on the information in this zine. You can contact her for more information at How2AgeInStyle@gmail.com.

ACKNOWLEDGEMENTS

Thank you to my family and extended family for encouraging me to go forward with this project. Thanks also to all the people who read and gave feedback on this zine as it was developing and to my younger friends who constantly challenged me to change my way of thinking! Finally, thanks to the editing team at Microcosm, who were amazing guides throughout my learning of how to put this zine together

SUBSCRIBE!

For as little as $15/month, you can support a small, independent publisher and get every book that we publish—delivered to your doorstep!

www.Microcosm.pub/BFF